Teen Sex, Pitfalls and Possibilities

Sylvester H. Edwards Sr.

ISBN: 979-8-9859936-0-8

All Scripture references are taken
from the Holy Bible King James Version

Copyright notice by Sylvester H. Edwards Sr.

The above information forms this copyright notice

Copyright © 2021 by Sylvester H. Edwards Sr.

All rights reserved. No part of this book may be reproduced, scanned, or distributed in any printed or electronic form without permission.

Topics of Conversation

Introduction	1
Challenges	3
Provide	7
Abortion	11
Protection	17
Trials and Stumbling Blocks	21
Working Things Out Together	25
New Relationships	33
Child Support/Court	37
Single Parenthood	41
God	47
Know Your Child	49
Thanks	53
Unexpected Thank You	55
Giving Back	59

Introduction

In the previous book, we dealt with some of the decisions, experiences, and outcomes of teens who decide to engage in sexual activity. As we discussed them, we found that many things can happen as a result of that one decision. In this book, I want to share with you some of the pitfalls and possibilities that can arise when you are a teen parent as a result of your decision to engage in teen sex. Some of the challenges are tough to deal with, and a true challenge to overcome. The pitfalls cannot be labeled as general to all as every parenting situation is unique. The possibilities and pitfalls are heavily dependent on the decisions the parents make for the child and themselves. I hope that you will find this book helpful and informative as it is written to open your understanding to the things that are often involved in parenting. The topics of conversation are topics that are not usually spoken about before sex and often not spoken of during the pregnancy, but should be spoken of in conversation as soon as the pregnancy is realized. The earlier you begin the conversation about the welfare of the child and the relationship of the parents the easier it will be to make the right decisions and make them together. Teens and young adults alike often make the decisions without hearing some of the experiences that can lie ahead when decisions are made. I believe that this book will help someone realize the responsibilities of parenting, and more importantly, the responsibilities of deciding to engage in sex before marriage especially as a teenager. It is so much more than you ever expected.

Challenges

In order to raise a child as a teen male, there will be obstacles you will have to face. One of those challenges is being a father from teen to adult. In order to properly speak on this topic, I will need to use much of my own experience. As a teen father, I found myself in constant thought while under constant pressure. It was the mid 80's and I was now faced with the questions; "Who am I? Who am I going to be? What kind of father will I become? Can I make it? Who can I turn to?" Often, the confusion from all of the questions left me in deep thought about how I would find the answers. As a teen, most of the answers seem out of reach. I mean they seem like they are too hard to reach, or things simply are not going to work out well for you. Picture this, a sixteen-year-old father with a part-time job raising a baby girl. Just the sound of it now makes me shake my head at how it all turned out and the process I endured. So back to the struggle of it all, I found myself in a bad place mentally. I was not sure of what to do and I didn't have anyone I could turn to. Yes, I had my grandad and a mom that was like no other, but because I had decided to do this alone, I felt as if I had cut myself off from the world. It was my child and it was my responsibility. What helped me make sense of it all was; I faced each question one at a time. And as time went on, I found the answer to each question. Some from study and observation of my life and my own parent as well as my partner's parents. And some by trial and error, as well, some are through experience.

I had to grow up quickly and I had to be all that I thought my dad was not. Here is why; one day I was walking with my partner and our daughter and I saw my dad on his way to a Tuesday night bible study. I said "hello, this is your granddaughter." He nodded his head and kinda smiled. "I asked do you want to hold her?" And he said "no-no." I took that as rejection. Rejection from a man who I already felt rejected me has now rejected my child. I was angered and that anger I would carry for a long time. But I used this experience and every other experience I remembered with him as my motivation to not be like him. I purposed to always be a part of my child's life. Always, no matter what. Was it helpful for me to resent him so strongly? No, but at the time all I saw was rejection and I would not let it affect my child. Before I left high school I joined the Army Reserves. I was using that money as survival funds until I landed my first job. Once I secured a decent job, the reserve pay became a part of my budget. Again, it was not easy but it was getting better.

As the years passed and our paths went in different directions, I found myself beginning to make a difference in my own life which helped me make a difference in my child's life. I worked a couple of jobs until I landed a job working in a warehouse. This was a more solid job than the previous ones with benefits and better hours. I began to build a life for myself. I moved into my own apartment, bought a car, made sure my daughter's needs were met, and all on 3.25 an hour wage. Yes, that was my hourly pay at that time, and with the help from God somehow it worked. Now it wasn't easy and sometimes I struggled more than I care to admit, but I was answering the questions that I thought I would never answer. I was growing into a young man with a path to success in mind. I had become a provider. Not just for my child but myself too. It was a tough reality to the struggle, my mom had endured raising six kids as a single parent. And I gained a new sense of respect for her. The main thing I learned was how to survive, and the proper way to provide, with love as my motivation.

As for my dad, it took many years for us to find a common ground reason to talk. After the refusal to hold his grandchild, I really didn't care if we ever talked again. I realized as the years passed, and I talked more with my mom that he experienced a lot just like we did. It was his marriage that failed, and his efforts to provide with love were misunderstood by me. It took us talking when I was twenty-five, and me asking a hard question that made it all clear to me. He was a good dad in his own way, for his reasons powered by his own motivation and love. I listened and learned that there are more sides to a story than one can tell. I used that first talk to change the future for myself and my kids and my dad. We began a relationship from where we were and we have grown even closer everyday.

Provide

Being a good provider means more than money, but time, effort, and love. Being there to share your time is crucial. As you share your time, you will be asked questions and given opportunities to teach as your answer. Sometimes the same question may be asked more than once, but you are there and can answer them every time. When my daughters were small the oldest would ask a lot of questions. There was one question she asked every time we crossed the bridge toward the downtown area. "Daddy, what's that building?" Every time she asked, I answered. I never said you asked that before or many times already. I never asked don't you remember what I told you the last time? I never got tired of answering because I was happy she looked to me as one who could answer her questions. Answering the questions of your child builds trust, confidence, and knowledge.

Time is also well spent playing games and taking trips. Maybe small trips around your city to learn more about life and having fun is a great way to spend some time with them. It could mean putting them in bed and reading a book to them every night. Sounds like a task or even like it may be boring but I promise you, it will be so much more enjoyable than you think. What you share at that time will be so much more than a story. But a special bond and a time of small conversation. In other words, what you will share is your time. Time is more important than the money you give or the promises you make. When a child grows they will require finances for different reasons. Yes, you are responsible to make sure those things are taken care of, but that is not taking care of the child. The child needs every area of care from you. They need your help and advice. They need your knowledge to create. They need discipline and your trust. Notice none of the things I just mentioned had anything to do with money. You have to be ready to provide everything in every area of care that they will need when they need it. Sometimes it will seem like they don't need you much at all. That is to be expected and is a sign that they are growing into the person they will become. It's also a sign that they are learning from you and applying the lessons they are learning from you. Keep teaching, keep sharing of yourself your finances, and your time. Time will prove it. It will be one of the best decisions you made as a parent.

Sharing your time with them is sharing yourself with them. Sharing yourself with them is sharing your effort with them. Kids need you around to be their provider and protector but they also need you to be there for them and with them. They need you to share who you are with them while sharing your time with them. Kids look to learn from their parents and truthfully, that's who they should learn from the most. You are the example to them of what a father is, what a man is, what a friend is, what a dad should be, and even what a husband is. You may say but I am only in my early twenties how can I be all of that? It's a learning process. Just like they are growing into who they will become you are developing into the example they will see and learn to be in every area of life. It may be a bit scary and that is not a bad thing. Use the fear you have to encourage yourself to be your best and do your best at all times.

To share your love is the most important and most involved sharing you will ever do. It may seem like it is not so involved, but it should be involved in everything you do. The sharing of your time and the sharing of your effort, all fall within the sharing of your love. But know it goes much farther than that. Sharing your love as a teen dad growing into an adult dad will be a learning curve for you while being a memorable time for the child. When I was developing into a young adult from being a teen dad, I found myself learning how to devote my time, how to apply discipline to my own life while learning how to parent, and the many different things that I did not know about my child's mother, our efforts together, what a child requires and myself. It became a daily devotion for me to study the process while living the process. I learned to adjust the things I did according to the happenings of the day to be sure my decisions were the best decisions for my children and myself. I learned to share myself with them. And in doing so,

I learned to love them in the ways that they needed me to. Some days the love would require more time than I expected and some days it would require more effort but every day and every night it required my love. And every day, I gave all that I had. What I found out was that the more I gave, the more I received in return from them. And though I was no longer in a relationship with their mom I saw us getting along, sharing and caring for each other in a new way as better friends. Love is not limited to what you feel, it is non-conformable. Yet able to be conformed into so many different things that are needed in parenting a child. Be ready and be sure you stay open to the changing needs of your child and be sure you change with them. Trust me it will be so much more rewarding than you expect.

Abortion

Abortions are a sore subject to discuss. But before we explore this topic, I first want it to be known that I do not believe in abortion. I believe every child can be born and can be cared for and loved, even by a family that adopts the child. A family member of a man and a woman will always be the best family to raise a child. Single parents can be a great child-rearing force as well. Yet It adds extra pressures on the single parent to succeed without the help of a helpmate. The experience of being in a place of decision for a parent is hard. The everyday decisions of love and care carry a lot of weight. Yet the hardest decision to make for many is whether to keep the child or not. When this decision has to be made, many options must be considered. Adoption, giving up all rights to a family member, the governmental child system, and then there is abortion. This option so often seems like the easiest and the fastest way to resolve an unexpected, and sometimes unwanted pregnancy. But the truth is it is the worst of all of the options. Abortion causes death in more than one way.

First, the death of the unborn child. Yes, the child that is conceived begins to live at conception. No different than you did when you were conceived, they grow and thrive in the process of development as they live in the womb. It is a hard decision to make and to go through with the decision of abortion for both the mother and the father of the child. For the mother, it becomes a physical, emotional, and mental challenge. Physically it ends the pregnancy and also the life of the child. Physically it can cause damage to the body of the mother that may not manifest immediately and can be a lifelong issue for her. Physically she will have to allow someone to alter her body and its functions that will affect her in other ways. The next way is emotional. Emotionally, this decision is a heavy one, and it will weigh heavy for a long time. She is left to deal with the emotional effects of the decision and the procedure as alone as no one can share in that with her. Crying unexpectedly and even uncontrollably because of the emotional weight of the decision made may happen. Emotionally, she may need to see a professional who will help her deal with the stresses of the decision she has made. Emotionally, she may make decisions that will affect other areas of her life because of the decision made to abort the child.

The next is that it can contribute to mental death as it affects her mentally. Mentally, she has to endure the decision and the procedure. It becomes a memory that cannot be forgotten. In times when she least expect it, the memory can often come to the forefront of her mind, and she re-lives the experience over and over again. Emotionally, she can be affected in a way that will negatively affect the relationship she has with the father of the child as well as other relationships she may have in her future. Mentally she can blame herself and the father of the child. It can become a horrible way for her to live. Did I make the right decision? Have I ruined my life spiritually? Is my worth diminished because of the experience of aborting the child? So many questions and little answers can emotionally bring her to a place of shame. This experience and the aftermath of it will often leave scars for life. Again she will need to see a professional who will help her deal with the emotional pressures of the decision and the experience.

For him, it becomes almost the same challenge as it is for her. Now I must admit that many men have forced women, and helped women financially and mentally make the decision and endure the procedure. Even provided transportation to the clinic for the procedure with empty promises of support. It is usually done from his perspective as a way of dodging the responsibility of being a parent. As well, it is a way of him ensuring that she does not change her mind. Over time it became a go-to method for many, and now it is a political issue yet to be settled. So back to the dad's challenge. He has to deal with the emotional decision to abort as the mom does, but with a different perspective. He has to emotionally deal with his feelings of deciding not to parent the child. His feelings of pain and anguish from his decision and his support of the decision. He too may find himself crying at times and needing the help of a professional to deal with the emotional weight of the decision. His heart will ache the same as the moms for the loss of life that he helped create. Mentally, he will have to deal with the questions; was it a boy child, his legacy? Was it a girl that would have been his princess? Did I make the right decision? How does this affect my spiritual life? These questions and more will enter his mind time after time, and he may deal with them for the rest of his life. He too can experience a level of mental death. He can equally experience the residual reminders from the emotional scars that many carry for life. He can also benefit from the help of a professional to deal with the decisions he has made. Most guys will try to be strong and macho and deal with these challenges without sharing and trusting a professional to help them, but I would recommend that he use every resource in his reach to help him deal with the decision. And for some, the experience has now altered their lives.

In the end, they both will have to recognize that they have decided to stop life from coming into the world. Stopped a child from growing, learning, and experiencing life while developing into a productive part of society. Made the decision that carries more responsibility than expected and more weight than can be imagined. Each case is different, and each set of parents will react, respond, and remember differently. Yet each will remember and have to deal with the emotional, mental, and physical aspects of the decision made. Note that this is not all that is involved in deciding to abort a child but a short description of the things that often must be dealt with when the decision is made. Before considering abortion, ask yourself if it is worth it to abort the child?

Often a death not spoken is when the mother has the child and one or both parents play a part in killing the child. Physical death is not abortion but it is a method of death that must be addressed. When parents decide to have a child, they have decided to take on the responsibility of raising the child. This decision begins when they decide to have sex. Yet so many find themselves overwhelmed when the child is born and decide to try to get rid of the child. Let me stop here and say even an unwanted child that has been born can be put up for adoption or given to a family member to raise. Murdering the child should never become a thought in your mind. Please let the child live.

Protection

So, the hard truth is that you would not be deciding to abort or not had you decided to use protection I understand that the use of protective measures does not equate to one hundred percent protection. Yet the fact remains that most times, it is the misuse of the protective measure that fails, and not the measure itself. So let's look at a few of the popular protection methods available today. Condoms: One of the easiest to obtain and one of the easiest to use, yet so many chose to skip the use for personal preference of feel over protection. I was one of those who chose to not use the protection available because of my personal preference. I used the excuse that I could not afford it. Well, could I afford the child that would be conceived from the lack of protection? No. The next excuse is it lessons the feel and enjoyment during sex. So how does it feel being a teen parent? Was it worth the lack of protection choice you made? Are you enjoying the pressure and experience as a teen? No. Then there is the blame excuse. She said she was on birth control. So did that work for you when you found out that she missed a couple of pills not always a fault of her own? No. Yes, sometimes women forget, sometimes they have negative reactions to the pills and have to be prescribed a different one. If your choice to not protect falls in these times, your chance to become pregnant as a teen increases dramatically. Remember it is not just the teen female who is pregnant but the teen male as well. To be fair, I will say that some young ladies intentionally deceive young men. But by the same token, so many young men intentionally deceive the young ladies by walking away and not sharing in the responsibility of parenting. One does not equate or cancel the other out, and neither is the right decision for the child. The right decision would be to choose not to save sex until after marriage. Yet so many of us don't choose that choice, so the next best decision is to protect both people involved.

After my experience of being a teen parent, I would encourage every teen to talk to their parents or pastor or adults that they can trust to get the best advice before they decide to have sex. That may not be the uncle who is sexing every girl he can or the aunt who has a new male friend every month. It should be one who has morals and values in life that you see the fruits of. In other words, those who are on a path to success through solid decisions and a strong work ethic. Those who treasure education and desire all that life has to offer without short-cutting the system. Those who can see what you offer as a value and a future success story. These are those who teens should seek for council before making the big decision to have sex or any other life-altering decisions that you may be faced with. Just as important you must always consider the medical reasons to choose abstinence over sex and protection over no protection. Sex can be directly attributed to the deaths of many through diseases like Syphilis, Herpes, HIV, and AIDS. Yes, there are many drugs available today that were not available when these diseases began. Yet non of them carry a guarantee that you will live. They may help extend your years but without the diseases, your life expectancy would be so much greater. Some people don't get the diagnosis until years after an encounter. How many others have then been affected during that time, and how many lives were lost because of it. I know of some who found out later in life as their health failed and could not remember all of their sex partners to inform them. That simply equates to lives lost at a very high cost, the decision not to protect.

I will end this thought with this, the choice to not have sex has never created a child. The choice to use protection has almost always prevented pregnancy. The choice to risk it has been the cause of many ruined lives, the parents and the child's, grandparents, aunts and uncles, and many other family members who have stepped up to care for a child the teen could not care for. Don't let your teen years become what they don't have to become, parenting years. Make the right choice to wait and if not choose to protect. More than pregnancy depends on it. Your very life could be the payment for the choice you make to not protect.

Trials and Stumbling Blocks

This is so very important to understand, there will be trials and stumbling blocks as you parent your child. Trials come in different forms. Sometimes it's answering a difficult question, which won't get you out of a difficult place but will cause the difficulty to become more intense. Usually, this will be a question the parents are in conversation about or even a time when a new relational person is introduced. It may also be a time where you are faced with deciding to be there or be somewhere else that you desire to be, and the decision can be a difficult one. Trials come when the children demand something that you may not possess at the moment and you feel the stress of responsibility weighing heavy on your shoulders. It can be so many different scenarios of challenges that can make up the trials of parenting, but know that trials are strength builders. Every trial that you are faced with you will have to find a way to handle. Whether you decide to be there and forgot your other plans or whether you need finances that you don't have, and you borrow from one of your siblings to provide what the child needs. What you will find is that you learn to be resilient and you strengthen that resilience with every trial that you are faced with.

As for stumbling blocks, we must be honest with ourselves in knowing that we are not perfect. We are not perfect as parents, we are not perfect as individuals, we are not perfect in making decisions or in any other way. As we live and learn, we learn to do better while facing that we are not perfect. This equates to stumbling over the blocks of life that you will be faced with as parents and as people in this world. Some stumble over alcohol. This has been one that I have seen many people struggle with. It is not for me to say if it is wrong or not for parents to consume alcohol. It is my intention to bring it to life in this chapter so that it is known as a possible stumbling block, and it must be carefully decided whether to indulge or not. With that said drugs are also a major stumbling block. The use, sale, or distribution are against the laws of each locality and the laws of morality. I am aware that the use of some drugs is being made legal in some states but this does not apply to the parent's decision not to allow them to become a stumbling block. I will share this as a teen dad I tried a drug. It was considered harmless and the pressures from friends and family members convinced me to try it. My daughter's mom said something to me that made me realize that I was being consumed by the stumbling block. She said, "You don't need to do that and if you want to keep doing it, you cannot continue to be with me." It was a choice that I had to make and a choice that I needed to be presented with, to help me see myself for who I was becoming at that time. A teen dad with a crutch or handicap that would affect and probably was affecting my parenting of our child and the quality of our relationship. I chose to walk away from the drug and embrace being a parent and equally invested person in the relationship. Though the relationship eventually ended I always appreciated her caring so much that she confronted me and made me see the truth of who I was at that time. I did not stumble over the block and I hope you will make the same decisions not to stumble when faced with the blocks that one can be faced with in life.

Your trial and stumbling blocks may be totally different from mine and I understand that. Where you live, those that you are involved with, and the choices you make all play a part in what trials and blocks you may face. I hope that you will recognize them or hear the voice of those around you and allow it all to help you make the best decisions to successfully get past them every time they appear. Prayer is a key part of how we handle life's challenges and how we prepare for what life may bring. It is also something that we can omit when we are in the midst of the storm. The step-by-step success…

Working Things Out Together

The ideal situation and the situation most parents want for their teen parent kids is that they will work things out together. Two different categories fall under this area. The first is being a couple. It is so very important and vital that the child have both parents in their life every day. The best way is that the parents are together in a relationship. A relationship can mean a couple of different things. The first that comes to mind is being a couple that cares for each other, works together to provide for the child, works together to build a lifelong commitment and love for the family. Does that mean that you should get married? Not right away. Most teen parents are not mature enough, not prepared, and not mentally ready for the responsibilities and challenges of marriage. That is not to say that it can't work and it won't be successful. It is a reality that teen marriages are marriages that have a higher percentage of failure than other marriages. Please do not think that it is impossible, again it is possible and has been successful before, but before you make that decision, know that it will not hurt and will probably be beneficial for the two of you to prepare mentally, emotionally, financially, socially, educationally, and other ways that will be specific to your relationship.

In the process of preparing yourselves, you will realize many things about yourself and your partner that can help you be successful in your marriage. At the same time, you will be preparing your parents and family members for the strength, love, and commitment you have for each other. Sounds like a lot, and it is.. This is why it is beneficial to prepare yourself before rushing into an early marriage.

I must touch on a delicate subject of religious beliefs. Some religions may expect, encourage and even push you to get married. Others will ask you not to be a part of the organizations of the church you attend until after the child is born and counseling has been completed. I cannot say if these tactics are right or wrong. I can say that in my experience as I have grown in the church over the years that I have seen it happen and experienced a change in this process. Years ago, church organizations began changing their rules and practices when dealing with pregnant parents. Today it is still a specific religious belief and practice that is observed differently by the many different church organizations. Now here is the statement that may bring a bit of thought. I believe that disengaging with pregnant parents is the wrong thing to do. Yes, a change in their responsibilities and roles in the different areas of ministry may be the correct thing to do as I believe that the example for those in their age range and those younger should be a positive one which represents Biblical teaching. In order to achieve this, I believe we the parents and spiritual leaders of the teen parents should engage the teen parents together as much as possible with instruction, encouragement, and all of the positive reinforcements possible.

Your responsibilities in this area will be recognized as time progresses. As situations arise, you will be faced with choices and decisions that will shape the responsibilities you will need to meet. The teachings and reinforcements I mentioned before will aid you in making the best decision for the issues or challenges that you are facing together. I do not want this to seem as if it is a single-parent lesson. This is a lesson on you both working together to learn as much as possible and as well teach your child in every way possible. My mom always called those times "teachable moments" and she used every challenge or issue or happening to encourage us to become stronger in our adult lives. So you have to know that this is not meant to go until your child graduates or moves out but a tool you can use to help them for the rest of their lives.

The second is parenting without being in a relationship. If the relationship ends between the two parents, it must be realized that the relationship never ends between the child and the parents. At this point, it may be necessary to parent together while separate. That means it is your responsibility to parent the child together even though you are not together. What does that look like? For so many teen parents, it looks like it's normal for the mother to raise the child without the father being involved. This is a scenario that we see so many times, yet we can change this by simply being mature. That sounds so simple and it is. But we make it complicated by involving our feelings, wants, and desires over the care and upbringing of the child. We value ourselves, while the relationship the child has with the other parent has little value if any at all to us. Please don't think this is a woman-bashing moment as it is not. Some men are carrying the responsibility to be single teen parents and treat the mothers just as negatively as I explained before. The idea here is to bring awareness to what we are doing and how it negatively affects the child so that we can begin to change the statistics.

As a young boy around three years of age, my parents separated. And for a while, I did not understand what was happening. We went to stay at my great-grandmother's house and that's all I knew. As I got a little older and we moved into project housing, I realized that my dad was not moving with us. From about four years old, I wondered where was he? Is he coming home? Why is he not here? And that is what happens when kids have a dad and then he is no longer around. Even babies get used to their dad before they can talk they know who he is, and it affects them if he is all of a sudden no longer there. Again it happens often because the dad did not value his role as a dad and abandoned the child or the mother did not value his responsibility to the child more than her feelings and wants and cut him off from seeing the child. No matter the reason, the child loses out and suffers not being able to experience having both parents there. Sometimes, it's the decision made in order to protect the child from the toxic relationship the two would display if they were together. No matter which one it is, we have to remember that there is a child left in the middle of the two. So often, the child gets just that, left by one parent or both.

So you may ask; can it work? Can two parents parent this child together and equally without being in a relationship? The answer is a resounding yes. Not only can it be done, but it is the responsibility of both parents to get it done. It may take planning, scheduling, working together, and communicating but it is possible, and it is your responsibility. You will have to work out the details as it relates to your situation. You cannot follow what your parents may have done or what someone else says should be the way to work it out. Set aside your feelings, and whether or not, you are in a good place with each other and put all of your efforts into the upbringing of the child. Plan when the child will be with each of you. And that should be as equal as possible. Always considering what's best for the child educationally, religiously, financially, socially, etc. All of these areas of life and more should always be considered when discussing the upbringing of the child.

Here is an example. You end the relationship and discuss the best place for the child to live for school purposes. As a way of sharing the educational responsibility the parent that does not live with the child should be updated with all grades and school events and given the opportunity to share in them equally including financially. Purchasing the things that the child must have and what the child desires should be discussed and obtained equally. The child's medical appointments, school field trips, lunch money, and more should be talked about and agreed upon equally. You notice the word equally is continually repeated. It is immensely important that the full responsibilities of caring for the child are shared equally.

Not long after I became a teen dad, I had to embrace being there without being in a relationship. It was strange at first because so much was thrust at us all at once. Our decision not to continue the relationship, our family histories that seem to repeat the same thing over and over, our choices to enter relationships with others as well as our caring for the feelings of each other. It caused us to talk and realize that we both needed to give our children(we had two then) the best life that we could. Did we like all the decisions that others made No? Did it cause tension between us sometimes? Yes. It causes tension in our new relationships sometimes. Yet the need to provide the best life for the children was premier. I guess you could say we were mature about it. We discussed everything the schools said and needed. We shared the responsibility of providing financially, emotionally, and more. We even discussed and decided on what day we would begin Christmas shopping and often shopped together to share in the decisions and purchasing. By doing these things we developed a friendship that helped us raise our kids to become successful and responsible adults.

At this point, the best thing for you to do is simply to talk to each other and plan every step of the way. I am sure I said this before but it is so very important that you communicate beyond your feeling, thoughts, and selfishness. The life and care of your child is the motivation and the reason why this must be done. Will you disagree? I believe you will, but at the very worst you can agree to disagree and come back and discuss things again at an agreed time. By then maybe one or both of you will have new ideas to help you make the best decisions together. It's all about the care and love for the child while respecting and caring for the other person's feelings and beliefs.

Here is another quick example. As our kids grew and we parented separately, we shared all efforts and life decisions. If one continues their education, the other encouraged them. If one gets a promotion or financial increase, encourage them. If there is a home or car obtained, encourage the other to continue to push for success. We had an agreement to discuss what the kids needed and plan for it at least two weeks in advance. In other words, neither of us would demand anything in a right now attitude. It was like we understood the process of togetherness for the love and care of the child. So if the kids needed something, I would be given that information as soon as it was recognized, and I would let their mom know when I would be ready to get those things together. If one or the other person could not financially contribute due to a need right now situation, the other would cover the costs and be repaid later. That was a trust that we carried from our relationship into our friendship and it worked well for us. Let's talk about a more interesting and yearly challenge, Christmas. This was something that I prepared for in advance, and she prepare for it in her own way. I knew that November 1st was the day my monies would be disbursed to me and I discussed it, and we agreed to begin shopping at the beginning of that month and be completely done shopping by the middle of the same month. We had the kids make lists and we added to them as we thought was best. This worked very well for us and I hope it can encourage you to consider something similar that will work for your situation. Again it's not that we were perfect, but we were intentional about the care of our kids and we found ways to make parenting together while not in a relationship work.

New Relationships
(being an adult about it)

New relationships are a dynamic that can only be handled for each situation. The two parents are responsible to engage in relations with someone who is trustworthy, loving, understanding of the dynamics already in existence, and of a strong character. Sounds like a textbook definition, but it is what's needed to fully capture the full potential of success for all that are involved. When this happens by both parents the child is not caught in the middle and the newly introduced relational partners are not isolated from the care of the child. It also opens the door for the possibility of other children being introduced into the family dynamic. The level of maturity needed for the parents and the new relational partners is at its highest request for the sake of the child and the possible new child born into the family.

What happens if a new child is introduced to the family? Will it be a disruption in caring for the children? It can, but it can also be a positive experience if handled the correct way. Remember the child does not choose to become a part of the family unit, but the parents choose how to care for the child. It was when my daughters were about four and a half and two that their little sister was born. It was a new experience for myself and their mother as she was in a relationship that was going well. We had to then involve the child's dad in the process of caring for the children, which made the dynamics totally different for us both. It began as a separation of care in the respect for her relationship and the desires of the child's dad. I made it a point to allow no reasons why he would be made to feel disrespected by allowing him to father his child. I simply spent time with my girls daily as I had been doing, and he understood that I would come by and be gone at a respectful time. Their mom respected her relationship and their effort to succeed in every aspect of life. It helped make parenting together while not in a relationship possible. As for the new child's dad and me, we had very few uncomfortable moments. Sounds almost impossible in today's world and often it is. But it worked for us and a plan that is constructed by two parents to respect each other can work for today's teen parents as well.

As I explained this dynamic, I wanted to cause you to look at every angle that can possibly come into play in your family structure. You notice the family is used over and over in order to stress the truth of what is being developed, a family for the children. This family can be viewed as a single unit working together for the good of the children. Or it can be viewed as two separate units working simultaneously to see that the children are cared for but not necessarily providing the best care for them. Remember it is not about you, your feelings, or your personal desires. It is first and foremost about the care, provision, and upbringing of the children.

Now I want to address the relational changes. It is normal for man and woman to desire relations. Once you decide that your relationship was over and you took the necessary time to move on, it is ok to meet someone new. That needed to be said for those who believe that only the two biological parents can raise the child. The family dynamic of every family changes and is challenged with embracing new members. Even the couple who enjoy a lifetime relationship has to embrace new people into the family. Whether it's friends, coworkers, distant family members who become more relevant, or friends of the child. There is always a need to introduce new people into the family structure. The same works for the relational additions and they should be given the opportunity to invest in the wellbeing of the children evenly with the parent they are in relations with. Can they then cut the other parent out of the decision-making and care for the children due to marriage? Absolutely not. It takes the whole family unit to give the best care for the children.

Child Support/Court

If it comes to this, and I pray it never does, it will need your utmost attention and your full commitment. Just saying the words causes negative thoughts and feeling for me. I guess it is because I had to hear these words once and it changed my life. Not that it caused me to lose control, but it made me realize that I am not any different from the next guy. When I look back at it I never thought it would happen to me. I was a dad that thought his efforts were good enough. I was there for the sports practices and games. I was a supporter financially over what the court would have mandated. I made sure my son was mentally and emotionally alright at all times and did some extra things just to love on him. He didn't need clothes or shoes. He didn't need food to eat or a home to live in. He had more than most kids his age and that wasn't good enough. I ended up attached to the child support system and it bothered me greatly.

The child support system is geared to provide for the child, or so they tell you. It is statistically much more unfair to dads than it is to moms. Even the good guys who go to the court to begin making payments for the sake of the child often get treated like he has no worth. That is how I felt sitting in the mediator's office. I had always said that I would never need to be attached to that system but there I was and I hated it. What made it bearable for me was that I hired a lawyer to handle the proceedings for me and if it went to court he would speak on my behalf. Without going too deep into it for the sake of all involved, I will say that his expertise made me understand the negotiations and made the experience a learning experience for me to say the least. In other words, I found that things could be fair if I just listened to his advice, I did and it was fair.

So as I explain the child support option, I would recommend that it be only for specific reasons. A parent who has chosen to not be a part of the child's life for selfish reasons. A parent who chooses not to support the child in any way. A parent who lives well but allows the child to live in unfair living conditions. A parent who signs their rights away just to escape taking care of the child. A parent who lies to the courts about their ability to help care for the child financially to spite the other parent. A parent who uses the child support system as a tool to spite the other parent. Well, I guess the list could go on but I hope you get the picture. I believe that two people who can agree to make a child can converse and agree to take care of the child equally in every area of child care without the system of child support becoming their policing agency. What you will need to simply do is love your child and provide all that the child will need together fairly. This does not say that if the mother makes much more financially than the father that she should pay more. That is a selfish thought. Equal means we both contribute equally as we have agreed in every way.

For me, it was a conversation that I had with my daughter's mom when our first daughter was a baby. We had decided to end our relationship but we sat down and talked about her care. We agreed to equally provide financially and that we would share the custody of our daughter together. Again, sounds like a fairy tale but it worked for us. We agreed to not demand things last minute but to give each other fair notice when needs were approaching and to be the help if the other needed it. Yes if one was short on finances the other would make up the difference. It worked well for us as we raised three girls during a time when this kind of communication was extremely rare. Were there hard times and some hard conversations? Yes, but we talked and found a middle ground every time. When we disagreed we would give a little time and discuss things again. So I know that it can be done and it can work without the child support agency being involved.

Now here is where you can get yourself in a lot of hot water. Have multiple children by multiple women who all seek child support from you. Sounds like a mess and it is. What you will find is the system against you. That's how it will feel and that will be how it will be. How you handle the stress of the system will determine how you financially provide for your children. This situation can break a young man quickly. It will definitely challenge how you provide for yourself as your finances will be taxed heavily before you get your paycheck. Yes, child support is usually deducted like taxes and the court usually doesn't care how much is left for you. Sounds harsh and it may be but it is the reality of the situation. A lot of the time when you have to go to court, you will face the same judge and officials every time. If the judge seemed unfair to you for the first child, it will be the same for every child. Some have found themselves working and at the end of the week receiving a paycheck of a few dollars because child support has taken the rest. They don't care that you need to take care of yourself. All they care about is that you provide for the children that you have fathered. Sounds cruel and unfair. Look at it this way. You fathered these children and you have the responsibility to take care of them. Do it yourself and it can keep the courts out of the equation. If it's a bitter relational issue that you find leads you to the courts, be sure you are prepared with counsel. Also, be sure you keep a record and receipts of all that you do for each child. As my mom once told me "dry ink says what words cannot make a judge believe".

Single Parenthood
– making the decisions, carrying the full weight of care

This happens when one of the parents embraces the role as the only parent. So often due to a failed relationship and lack of friendship with their partner. Sometimes due to unexpected circumstances, which can cause a loss of life of one parent and even a decision of one parent to purposely keep the other parent out of the child's life. No matter the reason it is a super responsibility for either to embrace being a single parent. This means that every decision involving the care and upbringing of the child is made by you the single parent. Good or bad, the right decision and even one not so much right. It all falls on your shoulders as it has for so many that came before you. The question is, what will you do when the time comes?

As a single parent and parenting together, the most important thing you can do is to pray. Pray continuously for your child, their health, their path in life, their friends, and the decisions they will have to make. It is needed for every child yet especially for the children born with color in their skin. We have to begin to recognize that our responsibility starts and should end here with a prayer. After we recognize this, then the challenges we will face and the obstacles of life begin to appear a little less powerful to us. When we recognize that we belong to the creator of everything, the challenges must fall and victory in parenting is ours. I know it sounds like a preached message, and I pray you receive it that way to allow it to permeate your spirit and thinking.

Now that leads us into the next part of your responsibility, and that is to prepare your child's mind. It is vitally important that we teach our children the value of every aspect of life. One of the more prevalent areas is the area of mental strength. We must train our kids to know that they should see themselves as enough. In this, I mean enough to succeed in the workplace, enough to have the career they desire, enough to enjoy a lifetime relationship with a member of the opposite sex, enough to be a resource for the next generation to come. We have been taught over the years by others and our own people that we are not what others are. The truth is we are more than others are and we have to recognize that in ourselves before others will recognize it in us. Yes, they taught us incorrectly, and yes they operate a system that is built to keep us from prospering, but they can't stop us if we realize our strengths and use them to make a difference in the world. Will it be easy? Not at all. But it will be worth us pouring into our children and preparing them to excel in a world that is there for the taking.

How do we do this? Through education. Education begins at home and should never end. When a child goes to school, it is to teach them the basics of knowledge. But it is the parent's responsibility to make sure they learn the facts of life. Those facts are educational through home training, training on how to engage the public and figures of authority. Training on how to share love and how to help the fellow man. Training on how to handle money and invest in their future as well as how to use the financial resources to be a blessing to others. We must ensure that they know the value of true friendship and how to handle the letdowns and disappointments of life. We must become and remain a teaching source for our kids as long as we live. As they mature and move into the adult ages they will already be in control of their own lives, making good decisions and making a positive difference in the community and in the world. They will also become the teaching source for the next generation. That's how we can change the family, the community, and even the whole world.

I know this sounds like a lot and I agree that it is, but it is also needed to help our children prepare for and live their best lives. It is much easier with both parents who can talk and agree on how to approach these many areas of raising a child. Yet if you are a single parent you carry the responsibility of both roles the mother and the father and you are responsible to make sure all of these things happen as best that you can. Can you get help from others such as family members and friends of the family? Yes, you can and I encourage you to take advantage of those resources but be sure they have the same values and understanding of life and its many areas of learning that you do. It will make it easier for the child to receive, retain and put in action the lessons they will learn from you all. Being raised by a single parent I watched my mom struggle to make ends meet, struggle to teach her sons the things that a man should teach them, struggle to be a resource for us that others had with two parents in the home, and struggle to live her own life as a single woman. This struggle sometimes appeared to overtake her but with the help of my grandparents, uncles, and aunt that lived nearby we were able to learn so many lessons while being prepared for the life ahead. Living in what was called the roughest part of town and being subjected to every negative force of the time. It must have been difficult for her as she raised six children while working to provide for us but with the help of God she did it and we made it.

Now that I have experienced the pressures and pulls of parenting, I respect my mom so much more for never giving up. Never running away and never allowing us to be consumed by the world's devices around us. Did we have temptations and even try a few? Yes we did but because of our teaching and because of a mom with strong values and rules for our home. Because of a praying parent and the helpful resources that were there for her we made it. We made it out of the project housing and moved into a house. We made it out of the mentality of not enough and learned to embrace working hard and managing our resources to have more than enough. We made it out of a short life expectancy area of town that proved over and over again to stop young black boys from reaching the ages of adulthood to all living and becoming positive adults in the community. Without being the financial experts through educational financial institutions like some others, we did become financially mindful and now all live independent lives of prosperity.

God

One of the best things my mom ever did for us was introduce us to God. It proved to be the best decision she made for us. We lived for a while, one block away from the church that our family went to. It was her intention that we would grow up in church, in the knowledge of God and in the understanding of His Word. She sent us to church weekly and if we did not go, her rule was we could not play until church we as over. At the time it seemed a bit harsh, but now I realize her mentality. It taught us the importance of discipline as well as the importance of God in our lives. Back then respect and fear of the Lord were so much different than what is taught today. Your challenge will be to teach your kids the love and respect adoration and fear of God as a foundation for their spiritual life ahead. It will be the best and most needed lesson of their young lives. As well it will reach into the other aspects of life which will influence some of the decisions they will be faced with. If you were never given the foundation, I admonish you to seek a church that believes in God as the Father and the Holy Spirit as the spirit of God a comforter and guide. Jesus Christ as Lord and Savior.

Know Your Child

As parents, we must learn who our kids are. By this I mean pay attention to who your child develops into as they grow. As a baby, they begin to show you their outward changes, and sometimes they may look more like one parent than the other. But after a little time, that may change again. It may seem that every time people see them, they have a difference of opinion of which parent they favor more. Don't see this as an insult but look at it as positive information for you to use while learning who your child will become. As a parent, you will learn to see when your child does not feel good before they tell you. You will see the looks on their face and know when they are not telling the truth. You will learn the value of knowing your child and appreciate the effort you took to learn them. As well be sure to pay close attention to the different aspects of who your child develops into. Some will love one thing and then as they grow they will hate the same thing. My oldest son as a baby and as a child and even as a teen would not eat green peas or mashed potatoes. As he grew into a toddler and a young man he hated them. It was when he went to the basic training in the United States Marines that he learned to like them. Not because he wanted to but because he found himself in a position that if he didn't eat them he would not eat. So when we went to his graduation and went to dinner, he came to the table with both of them on his plate and began eating and I stopped him and asked where is my son? He laughed and told me how he began eating them and now like them. It was a learning space for me to see him adjust to his environment and embrace a change. I guess you can say I learned something about him that day. We should always look to see the changes in our kids physically, socially, emotionally, internally, and spiritually. As we learn these changes, we learn who they are which helps us guide them into who they will become.

Here is a quick help for 'you' parents. My mom always seemed to ask a lot of me and I always wondered why. One day I asked her why one of my siblings could not do what she asked and her answer was "I know my kids, I know who to ask for what I need to be done." Kinda sounded a bit strange to me at the time until she followed with this. If I ask you for what I need immediately I will get it immediately but your siblings may get it to me when it is more convenient to them. That statement made me realize that she had paid close enough attention to all of her kids to know them. Know what they would and would not do. Who to call for what she needed and who not to call and when. It made me pay closer attention to my kids and learn more about them. It also reminded me of a time when I was a teenager and

I had gotten fed up with the rule of the house because it wasn't allowing me to do what I wanted, yet it seemed my siblings were living free. So I called my mom at work which was supposed to be only for important reasons and told her that I was running away from home. Now I had seen enough television of that day to know I needed to take some things with me so I packed a bag. When I told her I didn't even want to take the clothes that she had bought for me, but I let her know that I would only take a few things with me and I was leaving. She didn't yell or change her tone she only said, ok. I hung up the phone and walked out the back door of our apartment. As I walked away from the door, the reality of the world set in quickly. I walk around to the front door of the apartment and walked right into it. When my mom got home she asked me what happened and why I didn't run away. I told her I did and what happened. She laughed and said ok. At this point in life when I look back at this, I realize that when she okayed me to run away she knew I wouldn't really do it. She knew her kids.

It is crucial that we take the time and make the effort to get to know our kids as much as possible. Not to control them and not to be unfair to them but to help guide them and direct them through this experience of growing into a positive and productive adult. It is not just what we should do but it is a part of our responsibility to our kids. You as a single parent or parenting together will have to do the same thing my mom did, she learned all six of her kids and it helped her get us to the successful places in life that we all have been able to obtain.

Thanks

Thanking your parents is something that I suggest we all do continually. As my mom lived after we were all grown, my thank you to her was for me to be a successful dad and a man she could be proud of. I used the words she said to me many years ago to help motivate me to reach my success. I came through the push to provide for my children while working hard to build my own life. It was how I purposely imitated everything that she had taught me through her actions as well as her words of wisdom that helped me make it. It was how I responded every time she called and made sure her requests were answered. That validated her knowing who I am. We all did in our own way what she requested from us but this was my way of thanking her. Now, we had some good conversations over the years and I verbally said thank you to my mom often but I believe the effort she saw me put into becoming who she hoped I would become brought her much joy as well.

Unexpected Thank You

After parenting and raising your child to become a viable and productive person in society through education and the love of others, there are sometimes unexpected thank yous that can and will happen to you. In other words, kids often come back to thank you when you least expect it. They remember your sacrifice and they remember your love. They remember the good times and they remember how you helped and guided them through their not-so-good times. They remember what you gave and they remember what you held from them, and how it was best for them in the long run. This is a lot to consider for them and for you, but their thank-you will be special to you. Know that it may not be a traditional way of saying thanks but it will be from the heart and specifically for you.

For me, it was different with each child. Here is an example. On my last birthday, the kids and grandkids who live close to me came over to love on me a bit. I was already in a happy place as my wife had gone above and beyond to celebrate me. As well my youngest sons had given me gifts and hugs that made me smile all day. When the older kids came in they had gifts and hugs as well. Then my wife's parents shared their love and support for me and it was a really enjoyable moment for me. At about 4:30 my wife informed me that we had to get dressed as we were running behind for another surprise. I quickly hugged them all and ran to change. As we left the older kids left as well and my oldest daughter said "Dad open this later tonight." I said I can open it now but she insisted that I go to the event and could open it later. I put the envelope in my pocket and went on. As I arrived home from work a couple of days later. I remembered that I had the envelope and had not opened it. I went and got it from my jacket pocket. I opened the envelope to find a note that started like this. "I have been waiting for a long time for this." I stopped in my tracks and read on to find that my daughter took the time to write a letter of thanks to me, for all of the years of parenting I had given her. It was surprising that she listed some times in her life that I had let slip my mind. At the end of the letter, I found a check of a surprising amount. I sat down on the bed in shock. My first thought was; I am going to give this back to her. I don't want her money. Then I shared with my wife my thought to return the check and she explained that I should not, as it would insult my daughter. It wasn't her intention to financially repay me what she thought the years of love were worth, but it was her heart saying thank you for always being there. For about a week I simply looked at the check still in shock. It was never my intention to be repaid. I only did my best to meet my responsibility to parent. Everything that I had done for all of my kids was out of responsibility for being an average dad. This was one of my unexpected thank yous, and it warms my heart.

You too can, and will experience unexpected thank yous from your kids. Sometimes it will be along the way of their growing up and sometimes after they have reached the adult stage and reached their dream careers. Either way, learn to receive from them as it will be their heart's way of saying how much they love and appreciate you for all that you have done and continue to do for them. The meals you share, the conversations you have, the privacy you protect, and the love you give. Unexpected thank you's are unexpected blessings that I encourage you to embrace whenever they come. I learned to and it has made me appreciate my children so much more.

Giving Back

(sharing with the next generation

What can you do to help the next generation of teenagers who may be in the decision-making process of entering relationships, whether to have sex, how to handle the stress of making these decisions and how to handle the results that can become life-altering? First, ask yourself what would you say to a younger you knowing what you know now? That should be the foundation of what you can offer to the next generation. So many times cycles are repeated because we are not given the information and truth of life from those who were before us. That means if we had been communicated with better, had experiences and relational responsibilities explained to us, or simply encouraged more intensely of the things not to do many of us would not have made the decisions that we made so early in life. As a teen parent and one who may be dealing with the expanded family dynamic, you now have much to offer the next generation to help them become the beginning of a positive change in the statistics of teen parents. Not only do you carry the responsibility morally but you are in the closest age range to reach them and have them listen. As for me, if I was advising a younger me, I would say don't decide to engage in sex because of your feelings, desires, or peer pressure. Stay in school and finish your dream to become a doctor. Begin your family life when you have prepared for it, gotten married, and also enjoyed some of the things you want to do in life for yourself. Again what would you say to a younger you? I say encourage the next generation to not fall into the same cycle of teen parenthood that you and I fell into. No matter the circumstances they can make it and we have a responsibility to try a much as we can to help them succeed. It will be worth the effort when we see them changing the statistics of teen pregnancy and changing the world as they grow and become the leaders of tomorrow. I am excited to see their future as I am excited to see yours. Remember you can make it to the level of success that you desire even as a teen parent. I am encouraging you to give it your all, and I promise one day you will experience some of the same experiences of gratitude that I have and even more. I believe in you and I am praying for your success. Go and be Great just as you were created to…..

Teen Pregnancy declines

https://www.advocatesforyouth.org/resources/health-information/unintended-pregnancy-among-young-people-in-the-united-states/

https://www.guttmacher.org/gpr/2014/09/what-behind-declines-teen-pregnancy-rates

www.ingramcontent.com/pod-product-compliance
Lightning Source LLC
LaVergne TN
LVHW051210080426
835512LV00019B/3186